POP DUETS for all

Playable on ANY TWO INSTRUMENTS
or any number of instruments in ensemble

Arranged by Michael Story

CONTENTS

Instrumentation

30685	Piano/Conductor/Oboe	30691	Horn in F
30686	Flute/Piccolo	30692	Trombone/Baritone/Bassoon/Tuba
30687	Bb Clarinet/Bass Clarinet	30693	Violin
30688	Alto Saxophone/(Eb Saxes and Eb Clarinets)	30694	Viola
30689	Tenor Saxophone	30695	Cello/String Bass
30690	Bb Trumpet/Baritone T.C.	30696	Percussion

Alfred

Alfred Publishing Co., Inc.
16320 Roscoe Blvd., Suite 100
P.O. Box 10003
Van Nuys, CA 91410-0003
alfred.com

ISBN-10: 0-7390-5427-9
ISBN-13: 978-0-7390-5427-7

I GOT RHYTHM

Music and Lyrics by
GEORGE GERSHWIN
and IRA GERSHWIN
Arranged by MICHAEL STORY

Bb TRUMPET/BARITONE T.C.

30690

WIPE OUT

By
SURFARIS
Arranged by MICHAEL STORY

4

SPLISH SPLASH

Words and Music by
BOBBY DARIN and JEAN MURRAY
Arranged by MICHAEL STORY

WHAT'D I SAY

Words and Music by
RAY CHARLES
Arranged by MICHAEL STORY

30690

OVER THE RAINBOW

Music by HAROLD ARLEN
Lyric by E.Y. HARBURG
Arranged by MICHAEL STORY

THE MERRY-GO-ROUND BROKE DOWN

Words and Music by
CLIFF FRIEND and DAVE FRANKLIN
Arranged by MICHAEL STORY

30690

MARGARITAVILLE

Words and Music by
JIMMY BUFFETT
Arranged by MICHAEL STORY

SCOOBY-DOO, WHERE ARE YOU?

Words and Music by
DAVID MOOK and BEN RALEIGH
Arranged by MICHAEL STORY

THE LION SLEEPS TONIGHT

New Lyric and Revised Music by
GEORGE DAVID WEISS, HUGO PERETTI
and LUIGI CREATORE
Arranged by MICHAEL STORY

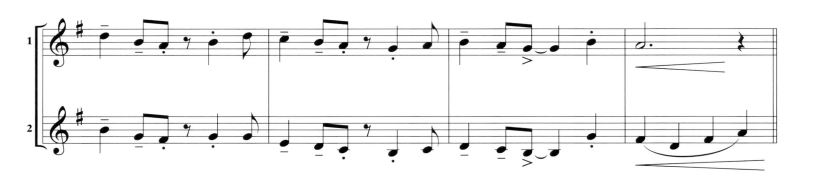

ITSY BITSY TEENIE WEENIE
YELLOW POLKADOT BIKINI

Words and Music by PAUL J. VANCE
and LEE POCKRISS
Arranged by MICHAEL STORY

30690

DOMINO

Words and Music by
VAN MORRISON
Arranged by MICHAEL STORY

(MEET) THE FLINTSTONES
from "THE FLINTSTONES"

Words and Music by
WILLIAM HANNA, JOSEPH BARBERA
and HOYT CURTIN
Arranged by MICHAEL STORY

BANG THE DRUM ALL DAY

Words and Music by
TODD RUNDGREN
Arranged by MICHAEL STORY

THEME FROM NEW YORK, NEW YORK

Music by JOHN KANDER
Words by FRED EBB
Arranged by MICHAEL STORY

CHATTANOOGA CHOO-CHOO

Music by HARRY WARREN
Lyrics by MACK GORDON
Arranged by MICHAEL STORY

Bright swing style

YOU'RE THE ONE THAT I WANT

Words and Music by
JOHN FARRAR
Arranged by MICHAEL STORY

RAIDERS MARCH
(From "Raiders of the Lost Ark")

By **JOHN WILLIAMS**
Arranged by MICHAEL STORY